A Compl

Kumihimo
on a
Braiding Loom

Kathy King James

Expanded Techniques for Making
Easy, but Elegant Contemporary Braids
and Adding Beads as You Braid
Step-by-Step Instructions Using the KumiLoom™
or Other Modern Foam Discs/Looms
to Create Round, Flat, Hollow, Square Braids

2nd Edition of
Kumihimo On a Braiding Disk
Expanded Version, Twice as Many Pages.
Includes Instructions for More Styles of Braids & Set-ups,
Instructions for Adding Beads as you Braid,
and a Photo Gallery of Finished Projects.

Published in the United States 2009
Primitive Originals
344 Creekside Drive
Leesburg, Georgia 31763

Photographs by
Bob and Kathy James

You may write the author, Kathy K. James,
at the Georgia address above, email her
at klaymaker@aol.com, or call her.
She welcomes any inquiries.

Kathy and her husband, Bob, operate an
online store selling supplies for modern kumihimo.
Visit PrimitiveOriginals.com or call 299-420-9982.

A Complete Guide to Kumihimo on a Braiding Loom

Contents

An
Ancient
Art

Introduction

In the early 8th century, when the Buddhist religion spread in Japan, people began to use colorful decorative braids in ceremonies. The making of these beautiful, usually silk, braids became an art, and later, people used colorful braids to decorate clothing, hang ritual banners, lace samurai armor together,

harness their horses, tie robes, and decorate their weapons.

Braids can be found in many cultures, but the Japanese developed the highest order of braiding techniques and complexity...elevating braiding to an elegant art that continues today.

Besides the usual traditional uses for decorative cordage, these elegant handmade braids are formed into competitive pieces of art, jewelry, or sculpture displayed in museums and art galleries. There are braiding societies all over the world that specialize in various kinds of looms and techniques that produce simple and complex, wide and narrow, flat and round braids. The art of handmade braiding still thrives.

Commercial uses for modern cords made by machine using the same or similar braiding techniques include every-day items like purse handles, necklace cords, drapery ties, pet leashes, sewing trims, belts, ski ropes, and, of course, the popular friendship bracelets.

The Marudai Background

Kumihimo (koo-mee-hee-mo) is a Japanese word for a braided cord... a braid consisting of 3 or more strands intercrossed. The verb *kumu* means to braid or to plait, and the noun *himo* is a cord. It was traditionally

created on a wooden stool called a *marudai*—a round wooden doughnut-shaped top *(kagami)* with four legs holding it 15-20 inches off the floor or table. The silk cords (or other fibers) were wrapped around wooden spools and draped down the sides as shown. Some marudai stools also have a square hole in the base, making it reversible.

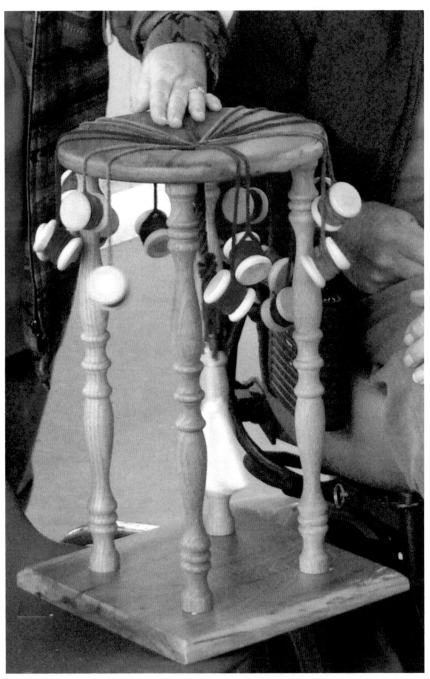

Lovely pecan and oak wood marudai stool handmade by Gerald Strickland from Savannah, GA. Curvy legs are removable for travel.

The Marudai　　Basic Technique

T he cords are moved back and forth across the ultra smooth surface of the marudai, inter-crossing the cords and creating a woven rope that drops down through the center hole in the stool. A small bag of weights is attached to the emerging braid to counter-balance the weight

Kathy James demonstrating Gerald Strickland's marudai at the Sunshine Gourd College, GA.

of the bobbins and thread. As you work, you release thread from the bobbins as you need it. A chopstick or decoratively carved rod holds the emerging cord steady when the marudai is resting. It is threaded snugly into the cords just below the hole.

When your cord reaches the appropriate length, it is removed from the marudai, trimmed, and given finished ends—tassels or metal clasps, for example.

Marudai vs. Loom Basic Differences

You might find it helpful to understand some basic similarities and differences between the traditional marudai movements and those of a modern loom.

When someone is creating a braid on a marudai, they usually move two strands simultaneously. For example, their right hand might move the upper right red cord down across the donut-shaped wooden top at the same time that their left hand lifts the lower left red cord up and to the left of the top cord. These two moves happen at once...easy since the stool is heavy and does not move as they work. It's a graceful and fluid move on the traditional marudai.

When working with a portable foam KumiLoom or other disc, you must split this fluid move into two moves—(1) upper right cord down and (2) lower left cord up—because one hand is already occupied with holding the loom steady.

An advantage of a portable loom is that you can easily rotate your braiding disc to keep your active axis of cords (reds, for example in the above drawing) running north and south. The marudai must remain stationary, so the artist must learn to cross his/her cords from different orientations around the circle of the marudai top. They learn rules to follow, like which hand is permitted to cross over another as they work around the circle. For a round braid, the next move on the above drawing is to move the blue cords the same way the red ones were moved (the blue axis). On the marudai, the weaver must move the cords right and left, crossing over their own hands.

On the KumiLoom, the same hand usually makes all the cord moves while the other steadies the loom, and the loom can be rotated so the active cords run north and south each time.

Tools
&
Supplies

Supplies

In recent years, it has been found that a simple lightweight kumihimo braiding loom can be fashioned from dense foam and notched, so that the cords are held in place by the snug notches, and weights are not necessary. A disadvantage is that fragile silk threads are sometimes frayed by squeezing them into the notches. Since so many lovely threads/cords are available on the market that are not so fragile, this shortcoming is outweighed by several advantages: lightweight, portable for travel, workable in your lap, inexpensive, small in size, functional without weights, and able to hold cords snugly when a work in progress must be put away till another time. In addition, flexible plastic bobbins are available to wind and hold your cords and prevent tangling rather than the weighty wooden bobbins/spools *(tamas)*.

Supplies   The Loom or Disc

A Kumihimo braiding loom or disc can be used in conjunction with plastic bobbins to create some of the braids that are accomplished on a traditional marudai. Actually there is a myriad of different kumihimo "patterns", from simple (3-strands) to quite complex (100 strands or more)—and hundreds of different color options for those patterns!

I've found only a few different styles and sizes of 32-notch braiding looms/discs on the market—each is white in color and has its own advantages and disadvantages.

 One product on the American market is a small wheel (3.75 inches in diameter) and round, scalloped with notches and no numbers. It is intended for weaving friendship bracelets and is sold as an educational toy. It is made of a 9mm EVA dense foam, quite sturdy. I found it to be a good choice for working with small diameter cords that are short and do not require bobbins (with not more than about a foot of dangling cord, since the ends tend to tangle as you work). It is neither my first choice for heavier cords nor for use with the plastic bobbins which seemed crowded beneath the small diameter surface.

I stumbled across another small diameter product (4.25") that was constructed of a thinner, more porous foam, intended for children's lanyard making. It has 32 notches and the four compass points are marked with dots. I found it too soft and flexible for most kumihimo braiding, as it distorted quite a bit when cords were stretched across the surface. It is better used for its advertised purpose...the weaving of lanyards. But, if you work gently, you can fashion friendship bracelets on it.

Both small discs appear to be designed/sold by American companies.

Supplies

I've tested three of the larger foam looms most suitable for kumihimo braiding (about 6 inches in diameter). I'm describing and reviewing three of them for you, including one of my own design, the KumiLoom™.

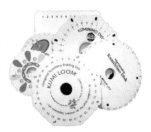

The 8-sided KumiLoom™ is made of a high quality dense EVA foam (similar to flop-type sandals), 12mm thick (thickest loom available), and is neither too stiff nor too soft.

It has 32 notches circling it that are marked with easy-to-read numbers at the base of each notch. A number is sometimes obscured by cords as you work, but it's easy to discern each number by the uncovered number next to it. The numbers are readable as the disc is rotated. The eight corners have compass markings on them —north, south, northwest, etc.—for flat braids where the loom stays stationary, without rotating. I found that this loom holds both thick and thin cords easily and comfortably. It is the least costly of the 6" looms.

As an extra touch, simple basic instructions with drawings are printed on the back of the KumiLoom, so anyone could pick it up and make their first braid. It comes in white only and can be purchased on the Internet by searching for *KumiLoom*.

Supplies

The round 6-inch Japanese Hamanaka *Kumihimo Disk* is made of similar dense EVA foam, a little thinner than the KumiLoom at 10mm, and I found it to be a good choice for Kumihimo braiding. It has 32 numbered notches, and 4 black dots to help distinguish four of the eight points often used when braiding. It is sometimes difficult to tell which number goes with which notch, since the numbers are placed to one side of the notches and some are placed almost halfway between 2 notches. It was a slight handicap when trying new numbered braiding techniques or when teaching others to braid. This initial shortcoming is of no consequence once you are comfortable with the braiding steps. This disk is available on the Internet in the US, as is its brother, a 6-inch square braiding plate used for flat braids. The square plate is of the same good quality as the round one and has better numbering than the round one. Both come in white only and are blank on the back.

The third loom, a 6-inch foam Kars *Kumihimo Disc,* head-quarters in the Netherlands and was found in an internet search. Round and white, it is made of a noticeably softer foam, and some cords tend to loosen as you work. I felt the softer foam had a slight disadvantage, since pulling the cords snuggly

Comments on Looms

caused the disc to bow slightly. Adjusting the cords occasionally alleviates the distortion. It is reinforced around the center opening with a plastic ring. Numbered nicely. Eight scalloped "fingers" protrude further than others to easily mark eight points. These are helpful visually, especially when setting up the initial cords. They come in three colors according to the Kars website. To date, I haven't been able to locate a retailer in the US. International shipping makes this disc expensive.

All three 6-inch looms/discs I reviewed work satisfactorily for kumihimo braiding. The two small discs/wheels are suitable for children's short cord bracelets made of embroidery floss or for storing an interrupted larger project when you need your regular-sized loom for a new project! The small wheels cost about half as much as the regular looms. I don't think you will be happy choosing them as your sole project loom, but you might like to have one in addition to the sturdier 6-inch loom or disc.

I tried several other discs made of lightweight styrofoam, wood, or masonite which were not at all suitable. I cannot, in good conscience, recommend them.

Your loom should last a long time, even with heavy use. And since they are not expensive, it's easy to collect several for simultaneous projects. If your fingers ever get dry and rough (in winter, maybe) expect the numbers to wear down a bit on your the looms or discs. You can touch up with a permanent marker if needed or keep your fingers softened with lotion.

You have the tools in this book for learning several braid patterns, some variations, plus beading as you braid. You will enjoy experimenting to discover exciting color patterns that come with different colors and textures of thread or cord and exciting variations in color setup. How you set up your cords initially will determine the color layout of your finished braid, so refer to the sample set-up pages. Enjoy braiding!

Supplies

I recommend that you read carefully through all the directions once before starting on a project... Kathy.

The 3 items you need for your first project in Kumihimo are a foam braiding disk, flexible plastic bobbins (8), and cords (8), each approximately 5 feet long (60 inches). I recommend half one color and half another. This length is for a necklace cord 16-18 inches long. If you wish to complete a longer braid, you need to begin with longer cords. The finished length is influenced by several factors: variations in the diameter of cords, the individual tension you put on the cords as you work them, and the elasticity of the threads/cords you choose. You'll find that although you begin with 8 cords all the same length, some cords seem to be used at a faster rate than others. Even if you use all 8 cords of the same cord, they still might not end at the same time (for reasons unknown)!

Supplies

When you choose some cords of one color/texture and others of a different type of cord, they will usually end at different lengths. For that reason, I usually add a few inches to my lengths.

The bobbins or spools are used to keep the thread/cord ends short and tidy as you work with them. If you've ever tried to braid long hair, you'll remember how easily the long ends get tangled as you work. If you don't have the flexible plastic bobbins, you can get by with cardboard floss spools and a rubber band, although it's a lot easier to just tug a little on the plastic bobbin to get another inch of thread than it is to remove or loosen the rubber band each time you need a little more. The 8-strand braid is so easy that most people want to move on to a 16-strand braid for their second project. You will appreciate 16 bobbins to do that.

The bobbins are made of a flexible plastic that can be turned inside out for winding cord, then flipped back to contain any stray ends. There is just enough tension between the layers of

plastic to hold your cord and still allow you to tug gently to release a little cord as you need it.

I find these bobbins to be useful for other things as well. Wire, embroidery floss, gift wrapping ribbons, shoelaces, artificial sinew, coiling threads, and more can be stored on them safely without tangling.

Supplies The Cords

There is a formula of sorts for determining the length you should cut your cords. Make the beginning cords at the very least twice as long as you would like your finished cord to be. I actually recommend you add ¼ to ½ again as much to account for knots, tassels, cord variations, etc. For example, if I would like a finished cord that is two feet long, I would cut my 8 cords 5′ long—2 times length (4′) plus ¼ more (1)=5′). This is a good length for most pendant necklace cords.

What cords or threads should I choose?

Besides the expensive, lovely traditional silk, some cord or thread options to consider are: satin rattail cord, embroidery floss, soft ribbons, chenille, "eyelash" or fringed yarns, silk cords, cotton 4- or 8-ply yarn, etc. Anything that isn't too stiff will work. Experiment with lots of colorful and funky options in the yarn department of your local craft store! (See next page.) Even wider ribbons, as long as they are soft, can be twisted as you work to make lovely braids.

Contrasting colors make striking braids. I recommend that you cut and use two colors of inexpensive yarn or cords for a short lanyard or keychain as your first project—just so you can learn the appropriate tension and techniques before trying a necklace cord. 100% cotton 4-ply yarn is a good choice, widely available.

Supplies

Getting
Set Up

Setup

(1) Cut eight cords (4 of one color and 4 of another) about five feet (60 inches) in length (drawing A). Grab them all at one end, stacking up the cords so that the ends in your hand are together and of equal length.

Tie one large overhand knot (B) in them, leaving 1.5 inches of dangling cords at the top after the knot is pulled tight. Make sure all cords are smoothly incorporated in the knot and none are protruding untidily from the middle of the knot (see drawing C).

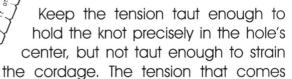

(2) Positioning the knot in the center of the hole in your disk (long ends on top and short ones dangling down through the opening), place your threads as shown on drawing (D), using notches 32, 1, 8, 9, 16, 17, 24, 25.

Keep the tension taut enough to hold the knot precisely in the hole's center, but not taut enough to strain the cordage. The tension that comes naturally as you work should be used throughout your braid for uniformity. When placing a cord in a notch, just lay the cord on the new notch and, without pulling the cord itself tightly, lightly pull the end over the rim and around to the back, then use enough pressure to get it to slip into the notch. That's all the tension needed for every move. (Remember, the first time around the loom is tight.)

(3) Now wrap each cord end around a flexible bobbin until the cord only has about 1-2 inches showing when it hangs down from the loom (see below) and close the bobbin. If you allow an excess of loose cord between the bobbins and the loom/disk, they tend to tangle as you work. Short is better.

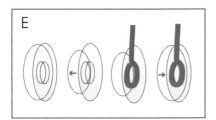

Wind up your cord ends by turning the rounded half of the bobbin inside out, wrapping the cord on it, and turning it back to its original position to close up the bobbin. (E) It will pinch and hold your long cord ends just snugly enough to allow you to pull a little and get more cord length as you need it, without wasting time untangling the dangling cords.

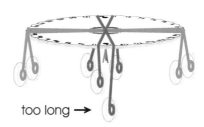

too long →

Setup

An alternative set up: instead of cutting eight cords of equal length, cut four cords twice as long as needed and double them. In other words, for a necklace project, cut four 10-foot cords, fold them in half (F), and tie them tightly at the halfway point with scrap yarn (or attach them to a metal key ring).

F

Continue with the rest of the set-up as described on the preceding pages.

This will give you a blunt end with which to work when the braid is finished (or a loop at one end for a keychain). Having a blunt end will waste less cord if you are making a necklace to which you expect to add metal endcaps.

Once your loom is set up, you are ready to make your first kumihimo braid.

Round Braids

Round Braid 8-strand   Instructions

The yatsu gumi, or 8-strand round braid, (whose moves can be done with 4 or 8 or 16 cords on this braiding disk) only takes 3 basic moves.

You will be trading cords repeatedly... a particular cord on the top for a particular cord on the bottom, then you will turn the disk so that you can do the same to the next pairs of cords. Here's how it goes:

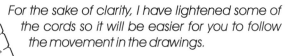

Turn your disk facing you so that notches 32,1 are up (or north). You should have two cords in each of the four compass directions: north, south, east, and west (drawing G), forming a cross shape.

For the sake of clarity, I have lightened some of the cords so it will be easier for you to follow the movement in the drawings.

(a) **Right Down**: Take the upper right cord (in notch 1) and move it down and to the right of the bottom two cords (to notch 15). Now you have one cord at the top (or north) and three cords at the bottom (or south). See drawing H.

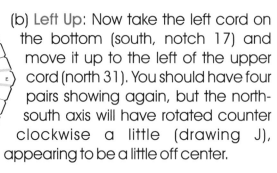

(b) **Left Up**: Now take the left cord on the bottom (south, notch 17) and move it up to the left of the upper cord (north 31). You should have four pairs showing again, but the north-south axis will have rotated counter clockwise a little (drawing J), appearing to be a little off center.

Round Braid 8-strand   continued

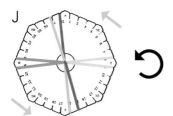

J

(c) Rotate: Next, turn the whole loom counterclockwise* so that the next pairs of cords are running north-south (or up-down). Notches 8, 9 are now at the top on this rotation (see K).

To help you remember these steps, say in your head, "Right down, left up, rotate..." After a few times around the loom, the moves become automatic.

(5) Now you will do the same 3 steps for the second pairs of cords.

You should have cords in notches 8, 9, 15, 16, 24, 25, 31, and 32. Notches 8 and 9 should be at top now.

K

(a) **Right Down**: Take the upper right cord (in notch 9) and move it down and to the right of the bottom two cords (to notch 23). Now you have one cord at the top, and three cords at the bottom (see L).

(b) **Left Up**: Now take the left cord on the bottom (notch 25) and move it up to the left of the upper cord (notch 7).

L

You should have four pairs showing again, and the new axis will have rotated counter clockwise a little (drawing M) making the cross shape squared off again. Keep your loom turned so that the axis on which you are working is running top/bottom.

M

* You can choose to always rotate the loom clockwise instead, as long as you are consistent.

Round Braid 8-strand   **continued**

(C) **Rotate**: Again, turn the whole loom counterclockwise so that the original 2 pairs of cords are running top and bottom (or up and down) once more. Notches 15, 16 will be at the top after this rotation (drawing N).

As you work, the hanging cords will shorten and a slight tug on a bobbin will release just a half inch at a time so your cord lengths will remain one or two inches long. (If you have chosen to use spools or cardboard cards with rubber bands, you will need to periodically release the rubber bands and lengthen the working cords.)

Got the rhythm?

You will always be following the same three steps every time the loom is rotated: "right down, left up, and rotate". Your braid will began to emerge (hanging down) in the center hole as you work.

Repeat these steps (a), (b), and (c) repeatedly, rotating and exchanging cords until you have a braid the length you like. You will have a spiral design, as shown.

Read the section about how to end a braid when you have come to the end of your cords. Also, I strongly recommend that you read over the next few pages of tips before starting your first braid. You'll find some important information there, including how to successfully stop and start again.

Round Braid

Round Braids

Using weights: Since the loom and disc work without weights to add tension to the braid, it helps to occasionally reach under and give the emerging braid a little tug. This keeps the cords from compacting right at the point of knotting. You can also create your own weight with a clothespin-like clip and some colorful heavy beads that can be attached to your clip.

North, South, East & West: If you are using the Kumi Loom™, you can ignore the compass markings when producing round braids, but you will need them for making flat braids.

Markers: You can write or draw on any of the foam looms or discs with permanent markers. It's probably wise to put your name on it somewhere, plus you can place dots in strategic places if it helps you to learn or remember a braiding technique. The dots cannot be removed, so mark carefully!

Bobbins: The plastic storage bobbins are wonderfully handy, but if you don't have access to them, you can try winding your cords on cardboard pieces and holding it steady with small rubber bands. It's a bit more time-consuming during braiding, but a money saver. It is especially economical when you are teaching a large number of students—like scouts, a school class, or a weaving group.

Creativity: Round braids are actually hollow, since the cords never cross over the dead center of the braid. So, you could conceivably cover a pencil, by holding it in place while you braid around it.

Variations: By varying the starting colors & placement of your cords, you change the woven color pattern on your braid. Half the fun is playing around with colors and textures. You probably have a collection of scrap yarns and cords to try out.

Round Braids

Losing your place: If you put down your disk and go back later to work on it again, how do you know where you left off? For the Round Braid, look at the center of your kumihimo loom or disc. You will notice that two of the cords (blue in this photo) seem to be lying on top of all the others. Those blue ones are the last 2 cords you worked with, so orient the loom so that they are running top and bottom (up-down as above). Now rotate the loom as always and continue braiding. This tip only works with the round braid. Other types of braids work differently, but once you work with a braid for a while, you will come to recognize where you left off.

By the way, it doesn't matter which end of any axis is up and which is down when you start again after a break. For example, the above photo or loom could be upside down and still work!

Some of my students do this: they make the first move before putting away their loom...in other words, they do the "right down" move so that there are three cords at the bottom of their loom/disc when they stop braiding. Later, at a glance, they know right where to continue since there are three cords at the bottom.

Taking notes: I like to take notes and/or sketch color setups when I experiment with them. It helps to write down which color combinations work for you and which do not. Write it down soon after you work with them, so you don't forget. You can trace rows of circles using a small round glass or a quarter and add color lines with markers.

16-strand round braid
with beads (see beading chapter, page 65)

Round Braid 16-strand   Instructions

Once you know how to make an 8-strand braid, you know the steps for braiding a 16-strand braid or *kongo gumi*. You simply put twice as many cords on the disk at setup, and you will need 16

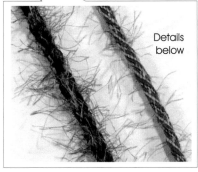

← 16 strands: tie-dye ribbon, black satin, eyelash yarns

bobbins. Your braid will usually be larger in diameter and of a more detailed design using so many strands. Of course, if you choose small threads, like embroidery floss, your braid will still be complex, but small in diameter.

Details below

Simply follow the usual 3 steps (right down, left up, rotate) that you used for the 8-strand round braid. Moving clockwise around the disk. Finish it the same way you do the 8-strand braids.

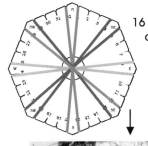

16 cords in 3 colors plus 1 eyelash yarn in the green E-W axis.

If you make all 4 threads in an axis one color (look right; E-W is a green axis), N-S is a blue axis, etc.) you can vary the alternating colors and get a spiraling design. Half the fun is choosing and testing com-binations of colors and textures of setup cords!

Round Braid 4-strand   Instructions

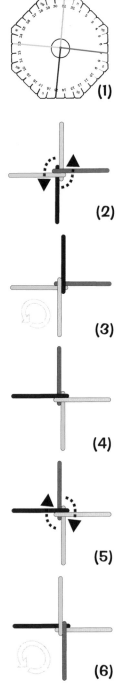

I've chosen to place the 4-strand instructions *after* the 8- and 16-strand tutorials, because the steps for this braid are so different.

You have two axes crossing, as in the 8-strand braid. Set up four cords on your loom, as shown (1). Here I used a cool blue/silver axis and a warm red/gold axis. For reasons you will understand better as you work, I prefer to use the flat sides of the loom instead of the points. (You can even use a square disc.) The notches aren't centered on the flat sides directly across from each other, so use whichever ones seem to keep your cords in a general straight line.

Your first move is to have the silver and blue exchange places on the loom (silver down and blue up). Think of the two cords as propeller blades on a helicopter—"spin" them underclockwise to their new notches (2). Then rotate your loom to the left (counterclockwise) so that the warm axis (red) is pointing up (3 & 4).

You will do the same exchange with these two cords, EXCEPT you must "spin" them clockwise (5). This is important. It places one cord crossing over the other properly. If you fail to cross them correctly, they will simply wrap themselves around the cords in the other axis. When done properly, the center knot looks like this photo. Rotate the loom (6) and repeat the moves—alternating between clockwise and counter-clockwise—until your braid is finished.

34

Round Braid 4-strand   continued

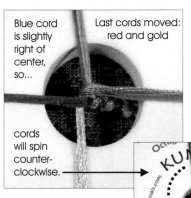

Blue cord is slightly right of center, so...

Last cords moved: red and gold

cords will spin counter-clockwise.

When you pick up the loom after taking a break you need to be able to recognize which way to move the cords (counter- or clockwise). If you look at the knot in the center, two cords will be lying on top of the other axis. Those are the last two cords you moved, so the loom should now be rotated so that those two cords are running left/right (East-West). If the upper cord is left of center, you will be spinning it right (clockwise), if it is right of center, spin it left (counter-clockwise).

Tips: I find that loosening and moving two cords at once works best. As I "spin" them, I keep them pulled slightly taut so the cords don't go slack. You need to figure out your own technique for moving them while keeping a grip on your loom at the same time.

IMPORTANT: I've discovered that you can produce a much more even and smooth braid if you clamp or tie a little weight on the emerging braid. The 4-strand round braid (which is not hollow like the 8- or 16-strand round braids, by the way) can make a very delicate or narrow braid when one is needed!

Round Braid Setups

Blue-green ribbon, turquoise satin cord, eyelash yarn, and teal macrame cord strung with beads. See finished braid on page 76 and beading instructions on page 65.

Round Braid Setups

GUIDELINES FOR SETUP LAYOUTS:

(1) Lots of colors and random placement will usually result in a speckled or multi-colored braid.

(2) Filling every other axis with matching cords produces a spiral. See the "spirals" photo and drawing below.

(3) Placing large diameter cords in one axis and smaller diameter ones in another, will usually give you a bumpy or scalloped braid. Fun option!

(4) Thicker cords or 16-strand setups will produce thicker diameter braids.

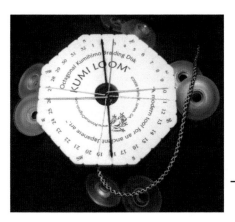

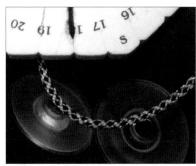

8 cords in 4 colors, black bamboo yarn, silver plus 2 shades of green embroidery thread

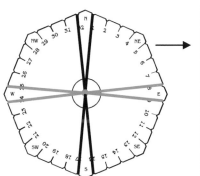

8 cords in two colors, black satin & tie-dye ribbon yarn

Spiral

Round Braid Setups

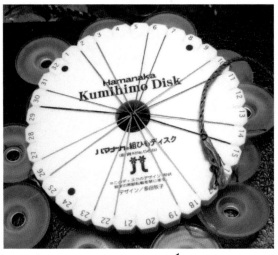

Speckles

16 cords in 16 colors
(shades of eight colors),
random layout, all embroidery
floss (split into 3 strands each),
no particular repeated design

Two shades of one color
can be elegant, too.

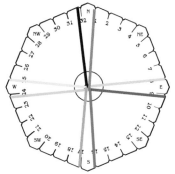

8 cords, all different colors of ribbon,
eyelash, satin, yarn, floss, etc.

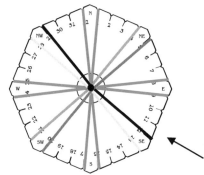

16 cords, chenille aqua, tan,
brick, silver DMC, one stand of
black eyelash yarn

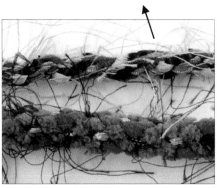

Round Braid Setups   Ideas #4

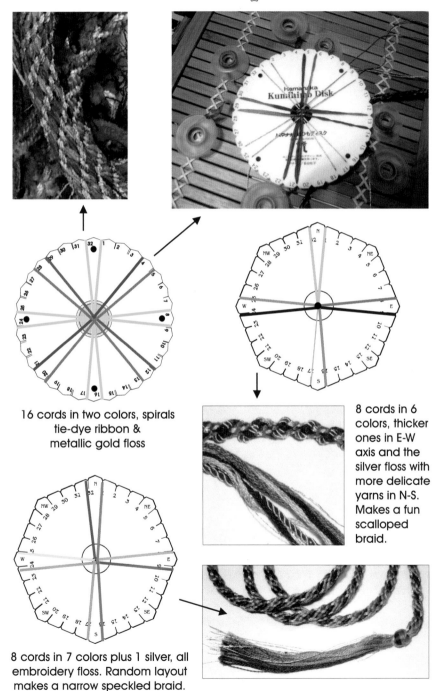

16 cords in two colors, spirals
tie-dye ribbon &
metallic gold floss

8 cords in 6
colors, thicker
ones in E-W
axis and the
silver floss with
more delicate
yarns in N-S.
Makes a fun
scalloped
braid.

8 cords in 7 colors plus 1 silver, all
embroidery floss. Random layout
makes a narrow speckled braid.

Round Braid Setups

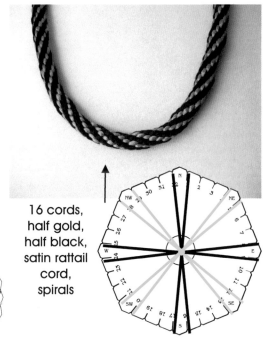

16 cords,
half gold,
half black,
satin rattail
cord,
spirals

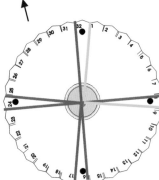

8 cords, burgundy chenille
and gold satin rattail

8 cords,
Silk/bamboo yarns,
copper metallic
embroidery floss

Finishing the Ends

Finishing the Ends   Tying Off Braids

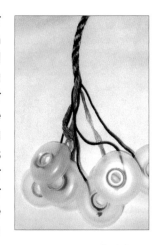

The final step is to remove your finished braid from the loom gently, taking care not to unravel the braid. If you plan to store it till you decide what it will become, then just remove the bobbins and tie the loose ends in a tidy overhand knot. Then you have a tassel at both ends. This works well for a belt or purse handle, or for temporary storage. It is also the proper ending for a square knot necklace closure with tassels. (See the friendship bracelet instructions, page 45.)

If you plan to add endcaps and a metal clasp to your braid for a necklace, you need to remove the tassels carefully and glue the ends into the metal endcaps. Here's how I recommend you do that:

You will need about 10" of a strong sewing or beading thread for each end, preferably in a color different from that of your braid so you can see it easily. The thread will be hidden inside the endcaps after gluing, so it doesn't matter what color you choose. There are two suitable ways to tie off the ends.

Make a loop in the middle of the thread by folding it in half, as shown in drawing L. Then attach it to the braid just at the point

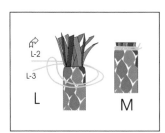

where the braiding ends and the ribbons dangle, and pull to tighten. Separate the two thread ends and tightly wrap one end (L-2) of the thread backwards, 'round and 'round the braid several times, then tie it to L-3 in a conventional square knot. Do this as

Finishing the Ends   Adding Endcaps

many times as you feel will hold it firmly without becoming overly bulky.

An alternative way to end the cord is to follow the same instructions as on the preceding page, except don't worry about looping anything, just tie the heavy duty thread in a tight square knot, wrap round and round, and tie again, as often as needed to hold the cord ends snugly.

Once you have your braid ends tightly tied, trim any loose thread ends and/or tuck them under the binding thread. I don't recommend that you do the next step until you are prepared to glue the endcap to the braid.

You will need good sharp scissors and a glue that is appropriate for attaching porous surfaces to shiny ones, like cloth/wood to metal or glass. Many super-type glues are suitable. Cover your work surface with a sheet of paper, in case of glue spills. Now, cut away the tassel ends just beyond the tied ends, as shown in M. Take care not to accidentally clip your binding threads!

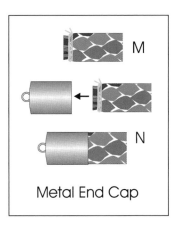

Metal End Cap

Carefully put several drops of glue in the endcap, following the manufacturer's instructions, and maybe a little on the braid end as well. Slide the braid into the endcap, give it a little

twist to smear the glue inside, and hold it firmly there for a minute to allow it to set (N). When you feel it's holding, you can prop it up on something where it can cure overnight.

Finishing

Kumihimo braids can become elegant pendant cords.

If adding a pendant, make sure the bail is the right size.

Slide your focal bead or pendant on **before** binding and gluing the other end of your braid. Bind, trim, and glue the second end cap in place. Allow it to cure/dry thoroughly.

Now add a clasp, using jumprings (metal loops). There are many types available: barrel clasps that screw together, magnetic clasps, lobster claws, toggles, springrings, hook and eye, and others. They come in many metal finishes.

Or you can just sew the pendant to your braid using a matching thread!

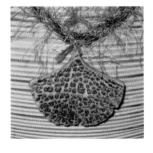

Friendship Bracelets   Instructions

Children seem to be able to master kumihimo braiding very easily. Embroidery floss, available in hundreds of colors and kinds, can be purchased inexpensively in department stores or shops where they sell cross-stitching or sewing supplies. It can be braided easily into friendship bracelets using the round braid instructions... either 8- or 16-strand instructions are most suitable, depending on how heavy a bracelet is desired.

If you do not choose floss, then make sure you use cordage that is washable and preshrunk. You will need 8 or 16 strands of embroidery floss. You can choose to use either whole strands of 6 threads or split strands of 3 each. The photo above was made of 16 cords containing 3 strands each of embroidery thread.

Square Knot Closure: I usually cut cords 20 to 24 inches long for this fastening method. The advantage to the square knot is that it will fit any size wrist or ankle. It is also aesthetically pleasing. Make your braid as usual, with tassel knots at both ends. Trim the tassels neatly to the length you wish. See square knot photo above.

Friendship Bracelets Finishing

square knot

Now fold one tassel end (shown in black here) into a loop. Weave the opposite end through the loop and out again, going over and under as you see in the drawing. To tighten, grasp all four ends and gently tug. Press the knot flat with your fingers. This bracelet can be adjusted easily for different diameter wrists and tightened again by pulling all four ends to secure the square knot. It also works well as a necklace closure when using a narrow braid.

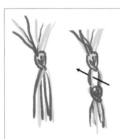

Buttonhole Closure:

I suggest cutting your strands about 18-20 inches long to allow for tassels, knots and the "buttonhole". Start by gathering your 8 (or 16) cords, tying the overhand knot, then splitting the cord into two bunches. Have a friend hold a pencil temporarily between the two bunches of cords, and tie another overhand knot, then remove the pencil.

This creates a buttonhole for the tassel knot at the other end. Now make the braid.

Using flat braid, next page.

When you think it is about the right length, hold it up to the person's wrist to check the length exactly. Finish it by removing the cords from the loom and tying another overhand knot. Trim the ends neatly.

Flat Braids

Flat Braid (Half Round)

Instructions

The *hira kara gumi*, or 8-strand Flat Braid, takes 8 basic moves. This braid is flat, but thick. Your set up is the same as for the Round Braid, two cords in each of the four compass directions: north, south, east, and west (drawing P). Turn your disk so that notches 32,1 are at the top. It can be created on either circular disks or square ones with 4 side notches.

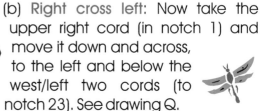

(a) **Left cross right:** Take the upper left cord (in notch 32) and move it down and to the right and below the east/right 2 cords (to notch 10), crossing over the middle and the east-west cords (Q).

(b) **Right cross left:** Now take the upper right cord (in notch 1) and move it down and across, to the left and below the west/left two cords (to notch 23). See drawing Q.

Same "chant" with the bottom 2 cords, <u>in reverse order</u> (see important warning on the Troubleshooting page.)

(c) **Right cross left:** Move cord up and to the left, from notch 16 to notch 26, crossing over the middle of the disk, and above the cords (R).

(d) **Left cross right:** Move 17 to notch 7, crossing over the middle as before. All four cords are now running east-west.

Flat Braid (Half Round)

Now, remember the four black cords that at setup were running east-west? We are now going to move them to become north-south cords:

(e) Right down: Take the cord from notch 8 and move it down to notch 16 (do not cross to the opposite side of the disk as you did with the first 4 moves).

(f) Left down: Place cord in notch 25 into notch 17.

(g) Right up: Move cord from 9 to 1.

(h) Left up: Move cord from 24 to 32.

(I) Now, before starting over with the 8 steps, adjust your east-west cords. Move them back to slots 24, 25, 8, and 9. See (U).

Repeat all the steps until you run out of cord or your cord has reached the length you like. Remove all cords from the disk, remove bobbins, and tie an overhand knot in the loose ends. Or finish it off as desired.

HIRA CAN HELP YOU REMEMBER THE STEPS: Your cords represent Hira (pronounced here-ruh), a dragonfly at rest (see P). He puts his antennas back and to the sides in preparation to fly (Q).Next he pulls in his legs (R) and takes off with his wings wide! Ready to land again, he puts his feet back down first (S), then his antenna forward (T), lands again, and closes his wings (U)!

Flat Braids

This braid <u>works best if all your cords are the same</u> texture and size. Make sure you familiarize yourself with the Setup Key so you can design your own flat braid combinations!

When working this flat braid, you will notice that the <u>cords tend to lean to the South in the hole</u>. This is normal and you will get used to it. Also the two cords to the South get slack during some of the moves. Avoid trying to adjust them...just keep making the moves and you will see that the slack is taken up again in the next moves.

Keep the same <u>even tension throughout a braid</u>, not too tight and not too loose. Overtight braids tend to be stiff. (This is true of all the braiding techniques in this book.) Tying a weight underneath on the emerging might help keep your tension even.

The fanciful story of **Hira** at the bottom of the instructions can be really helpful for keeping you on track. This is especially helpful for those students who learn best using visual tactics, even imaginary ones. Give it a try!

NOTICE! There is one move in the instructions where a mistake is easily made. When moving from notch 16 to 26, in (c) right cross left, make sure that you never accidently do "left cross right" before "right cross left". The design will change and it is difficult to undo!

A mental trick: notice that there are 2 sixes in the move from 16 to 26 and 2 sevens in the move from 17 to 7. It might help you keep them straight in your memory.

Note, too that sixes come before sevens—that might make it easier to avoid the mistake mentioned in the paragraph above.

Flat Braid (12-strand)   **Instructions**

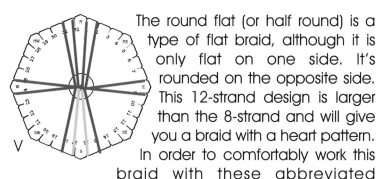

The round flat (or half round) is a type of flat braid, although it is only flat on one side. It's rounded on the opposite side. This 12-strand design is larger than the 8-strand and will give you a braid with a heart pattern. In order to comfortably work this braid with these abbreviated instructions, I recommend you try the 8-strand flat round first.

This setup can be done on an octagonal, round, or square disk (as long the square has at least 4 notches on the E-W sides). Set up on your round disk is as shown in drawing V.

(a) Follow the same instructions as for a flat round 8-strand braid for the first four steps, with a few slight position adjustments to account for the extra four cords: 32 to 10, 1 to 23, 16 to 26, 17 to 7.

(b) Now pause and adjust the top (north) and bottom (south) cords, by moving them toward the black dots (to 32, 1, 16, 17).

(c) Continue: 8 to 15, 25 to 18, 9 to 2, and 24 to 31. Now adjust cords on the east/west sides.

Continue with these steps until you have a braid the right length, or you run out of cord. Finish the ends as desired.

TROUBLESHOOTING: It's important to follow your instructions carefully. Crossing the wrong cord over another or in the wrong order, for example, can change the braid completely. Notice, one cord crossed out of order in this flat braid is obvious!

Flat Round 8-strand, 2 colors

Flat Braid Setups

"W" pattern using 8 strands; four black, four of tie-dye ribbon. Bottom four one color, top four another

Edges alternate colors.

Heart pattern using 8 strands; 6 pink and two red

Heart pattern substituting black for pink in this same setup

Coral snake design

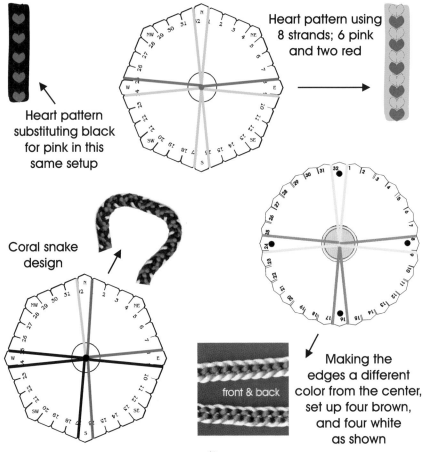

front & back

Making the edges a different color from the center, set up four brown, and four white as shown

52

Flat Braid Setups

Small braid, made of embroidery floss in two colors.

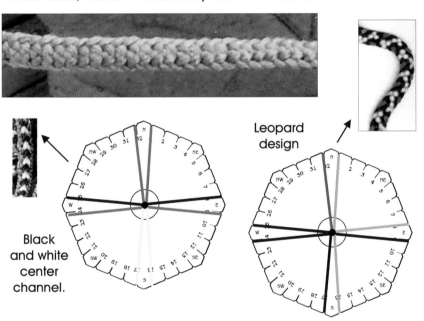

Leopard design

Black and white center channel.

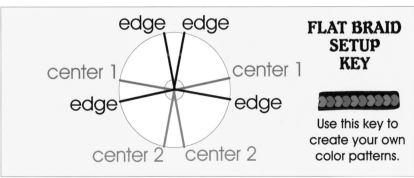

edge   edge

center 1   center 1

edge   edge

center 2   center 2

FLAT BRAID SETUP KEY

Use this key to create your own color patterns.

Hollow Braids

Hollow Braid

The techniques for this braid are interesting. You will make 4 moves clockwise and then the same 4 moves in a <u>counter</u>clockwise direction. The cords never cross over the center of the braid, so it is hollow and can even be pressed almost flat. It is the only one in this book that requires a weight to keep tension on the emerging braid. It can resemble latticework (like this project), spirals, stripes, or speckles—depending on setup.

A Tale of 8 Frogs

(V)

Once upon a time, there were 4 pairs of colorful frogs sitting on a lilypad, 4 purple girls and 4 red boys facing each other, as in (V).

Suddenly, the four red boy frogs, facing clockwise, leapfrog over their girlfriends and land on the next corner to face a new girl.

Not to be outdone, the four girls hop up and, leaping <u>counter</u>clockwise, jump over a boy to the next corner! Then they all wiggle around to get comfortable next to their new buddy. Soon, though, they will all get antsy and leap up to do it again—only to discover they are back in their original pairs on the opposite corner!

This moral-free frog tale serves a purpose...it might help you to picture in your mind the movements of the upcoming 8 steps for the hollow braid.

STEP-BY-STEP INSTRUCTIONS (story line is in italics)

(a) <u>Set up your disk</u> with eight cords in two colors, as shown in drawing (W), with cords flanking the four main compass points, N-S-E-W.

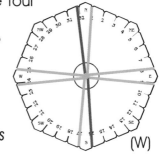

(Imagine that you are standing in the center hole. Each cord represents a frog, boys on the left of the compass poinst and girls on the right of the compass points. For example, the two dark green cords are two of the boy frogs.)

(W)

The hollow braid tends to bunch up a bit in the hole of the loom as you work if you do not add a little tension to it in the form of a weight. It can be something as simple as a bar of soap in a plastic baggie clipped to the tassel at the bottom of the braid. I have a small metal clamp (similar to a clothespin) that I clip to the emerging tassel. I add weight with a short cluster of heavy beads on a ribbon. Anything weighing several ounces will do. Beware of damaging your braid with your choices, though. Pins or toothed clamps might be rough on your cords.

<u>Clamp your weight</u> to the bottom of the tassel before beginning. Work where you can allow the weight and braid to swing. This adds a little tension to the emerging braid, keeping it smooth and straight.

You will be moving around the loom/disc beginning at compass point North, notch 32 (*a boy frog jumping to the right*). (Pay attention to the pattern of moves as you work so you can better understand which jump comes next.)

Hollow Braid

Always start the 8-step sequence at the top of the disk every time (North, notch 32.) *And remember that the boy frogs are __always__ on the left and the girls on the right of the compass points if you are "watching" from the center hole.* (Ladies, remember this by saying to yourself, "Girls are always right!")

(b) *First, move all the boy frogs clockwise to the next corner. See red dotted lines in (X). They only jump over ONE frog as they move.*

Start with the upper left cord. 32 moves to 7, 8 moves to 15, 16 moves to 23, and 24 moves up to 32.

(X)

Your loom should look like (Y).

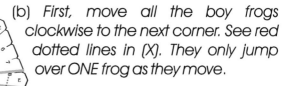

c) Resist the urge to pause and adjust your cords at this point.

Later you will learn that the gaps will help signal to you what step you were on when you put the disk away. So when you make the next four moves, ignore the gaps.

(Y)

You will NOT be placing cords *between* others at a corner.

You will NEVER jump over more than one cord (*frog*) at a time.

There will be no gap at North. Your spacing should be the same as drawing (Y) at this point. The moves you just made are four of the eight moves you need to remember. Let's keep moving!

Hollow Braid

(d) *Next, beginning with notch 1, let all the girl frogs jump* <u>*counter*</u>*clockwise around the lilypad, leaping over only one frog as they go.*
See purple dotted lines (Z).
Start with #1.

Move 1 to 26, 25 moves to 18, 17 moves to 10, and 9 moves up to 1.

(Z)

Notice that the cord you are grabbing to move (at E, S, and W) is the one in the middle of three cords and always sits next to a compass point.

Again, there's no gap at the North corner, but there are two empty notches at each of the other 3 compass points, E, S, W. See (AA).

(AA)

(e) Time to <u>adjust</u> (*frogs wiggle back into place*). You want all the cords to go back like they started, to the right and left of the four main compass points. Some cords will need to move left or right one notch to do so. Now start again!

Continue these steps clockwise and counterclockwise, adjusting after every 8 steps, until your braid is finished.

(BB)

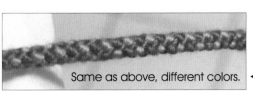

Same as above, different colors.

Hollow Braid

Setups

8 strands, four each of two colors, both of these layouts produce a spiral braid one spirals one way and the other spirals the opposite direction.

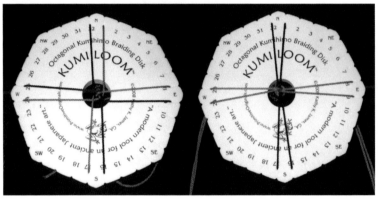

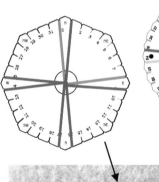

8 strands, in three colors, one black spiral and interesting pattern of green black and red between the spirals

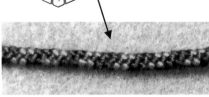

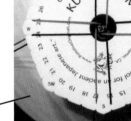

8 strands, four each of two colors, this layout produces a square-like braid with lengthwise stripes.

Square Braids

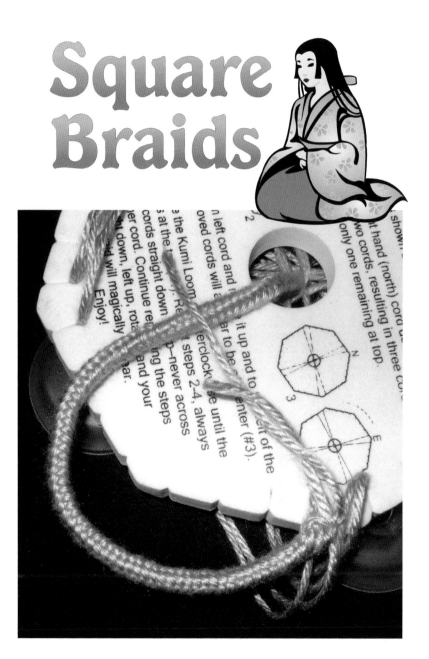

Square Braids

Instructions

This square braid is almost as simple to learn as the 8-strand round braid, and looks very structured and elegant. There are several types of square braids; this one can be set up on either a round or square braiding loom. It has 4 sides—thus the name square braid. I personally prefer the finished braid all in one color, since it shows off the repetitive pattern so well. To easily depict the steps, this first project is in 2 colors, and I added weight to the emerging braid for even tension.

Unlike the round braid, this braid doesn't rotate around the loom as you work. North stays at the top for all moves. Only N, S, E, and W points will be used. You will make four moves clockwise, then the same four moves counterclockwise, adjust some of the cords, and repeat.

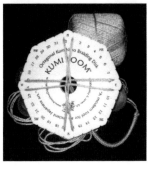

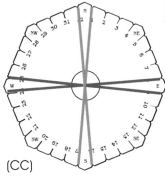

(CC)

Set your loom up with 8 cords 5' long, half one color and half another, as shown in (CC). Or cut shorter ones for practice.

(1) Clockwise, slide the cord in notch 1 to notch 7 and (the matching move) slide 17 clockwise to notch 23. Your loom will look like (DD).

Let's call the move "clockwise, slide/slide".

Notice that there are now three cords at East and at West. Your next step will move the center cord on each side. In fact, the only cords you will ever move from the East and West sides are the center ones. Continue to the next page to learn what to do with these two center cords (purple in this project, in notches number 8 and 24).

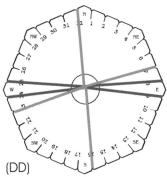

(DD)

Square Braids

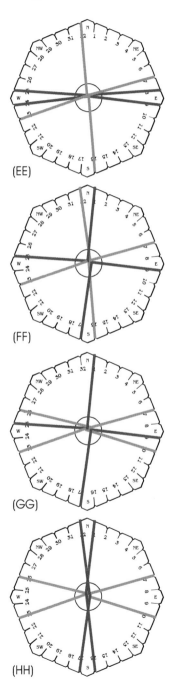

(EE)

(FF)

(GG)

(HH)

(2)Now take the cord in 24 and move it clockwise up to notch 1, where the original cord used to be, next to the N mark. It will jump over two cords to get there, crossing over the cord in notch 32. Then move 8 clockwise, jump over two cords to notch 17, and sit crossed over notch 16. It is now in the slot to one side of the S mark, which another cord just vacated.

Let's call this "clockwise, jump/jump".

Your loom will look like (FF), with crossed cords at North and at South. In fact N and S will always be crossed from now on when there are 2 cords there.

(3) Now we will change directions and move counterclockwise for four moves. Slide 32 down to 26 and slide 16 up to 10. Notice that the two cords start out beneath another, and move as if you are tightening the crossed cords (which you are).

This move is "counter, slide/slide", and the loom should resemble (GG).

(4) Now you will move the two E-W cords (in the center of the three), counterclockwise: 9 will jump up to notch 32 and 25 will jump down to notch 16.

This is called "counter, jump/jump", and your loom should look like (HH).

You are finished with the four moves (or eight, depending on how you count them). Before proceeding, you must adjust your E-W cords back to their original positions, flanking the E and the W on your loom. In other words, move 7 to 8, 10 to 9, 26 to 25, and 23 to 24. The loom will look like when you started, but colors are switched (JJ).

63

Square Braids continued

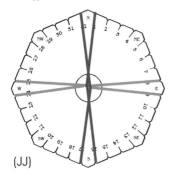

(JJ)

You are now back to zero, ready to go through the same moves again and again until your braid is finished. Remember that a weight suspended from the braid helps to keep it consistent.

If you work well using a repetitive chant, here's the one for this braid:

> Clockwise slide/slide,
> clockwise jump/jump,
> Counter slide/slide,
> counter jump/jump,
> Adjust.

REMEMBER THESE:

You'll never have more than two cords at N or S on your loom.

Anytime you are adding a cord to N or S, it will always be crossing over a cord already there.

Threes will only occur at East or West.

You will never remove any cord from the E-W positions except a center cord (except for adjusting, of course).

Cords slide into the E-W positions and jump into the N-S positions.

When you move a crossed cord from the N or S, it will always be the one underneath that moves.

Don't adjust till there are two blank notches at E and W.

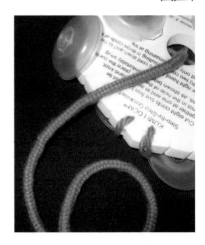

Beaded Braids

Beaded Green Braid   One Bead Strand

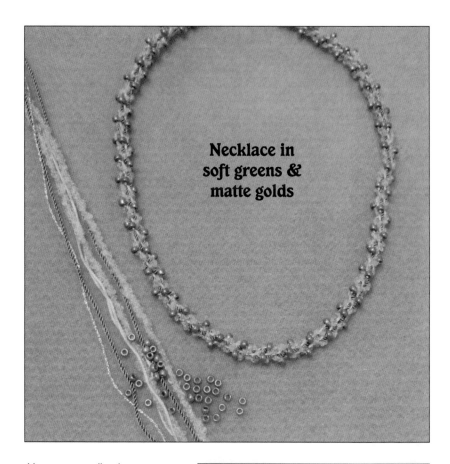

Necklace in
soft greens &
matte golds

You can really dress up a kumihimo braid by adding beads as you braid. This lovely soft green round braid has about 125 size 6/0 beads worked into it.

For this project I chose eight cords: 2 each of pale lime embroidery floss, a khaki baby yarn, an olive satin rope, and metallic gold embroidery floss.

Beaded Green Braid

Instructions

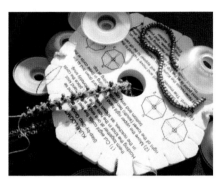

(1) You need 5 feet each of 8 cords to complement your beads. Cut one of the gold embroidery cords another 12 inches longer than the others. That's the one on which you will string the beads.

(2) You will need 125 to 150 size 6/0 beads—or any beads with hole large enough to be strung on one of your cords before braiding.

(3) Set up your loom or disc as shown in (KK), then add bobbins to all cords except the long gold embroidery floss which should be set into notch #17. Now add about 125 of your beads to the gold floss before putting the bobbin on the remaining cord. (I use a "big eye" needle to string mine— two needles welded top/bottom.)

The beads will go between the loom and the bobbin. Notice that this cord will hang down much longer than the others, so be careful with it as you work. I also clamped a little weight on the tassel end to keep my tension even.

(4) Since I plan to glue an endcap on each end when I'm finished, I don't want beads to be in the way at either end. I usually go several times around the loom/disc before sliding beads into the braid, producing anywhere from ½ to 2 inches of smooth braid before the beading starts. (See the braid to the right.)

To add beads, you will be sliding one bead into the middle of the knot each time the long gold floss comes around.

There is a specific place to put the bead for the best placement. The close ups on the next page will show you exactly where to place the bead in the center.

Beaded Green Braid continued

(4) As you already learned, when producing a round braid, the 1st step is called "right down". In the photo to the right, that step has just happened. (The layout to the right is a random point in braiding and may not match yours.) Now I am about to do step two, "left up". This cord from notch 24 has your beads strung on it.

Before folding this cord up and over the E-W strands, I use a fingernail to slide just one bead up to the center. I keep sliding the bead till it touches the cord in notch 31.

I then gently push the bead under the cord with my fingernail, so that the bead is between the 2 cords in notches 31 and 32. Once it is there I can fold the cord upwards and into place.

Be careful not to dislodge the bead. It should remain where you placed it, while you rotate the loom and move more cords in the usual patterns for a round braid. These cords will hold the bead securely in place as you continue. You should do the same thing each time you come to this cord... add one bead. If you are running short of beads, just open the bobbin, unroll the cord, add more beads, and replace the bobbin.

When you are close to finishing the braid, remember to do several rounds without beads so

the two braid ends will match, leaving unbeaded space for an endcap and clasp to be added.

Beaded Purple Braid   More Beads

This kumihimo necklace has two strands of beads woven into the finished braid. To produce this one, I chose several shades of purple embroidery threads and doubled them (two strands per notch) for six of the eight cords, plus one thickness of metallic gold floss for the other two cords (as shown below on the loom), on which I strung 125 frosted iridescent beads each. They added a gold frost to the finished look.

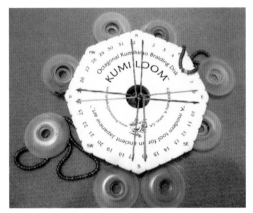

Beaded braids have a nice heavy feel to them!

Beaded Purple Braid continued

When setting up your loom or disc for this project, string beads on the two metallic gold cords across from each other on your loom (LL). Continue with the same instructions as for beaded necklace #1.

The more cords you string with beads, the more your braid will be covered with beads. But remember that your color cords will be completely covered with beads at some point and the necklace could become very heavy.

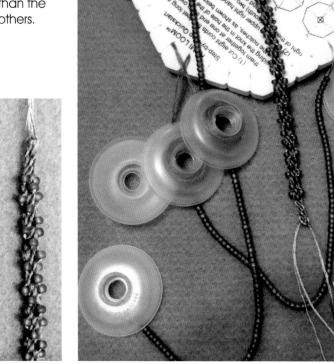

And don't forget that the bead-bearing cords must be longer than the others.

Enjoy experimenting with different beads and different saturations!

Beaded Copper Braid

8-strand beaded braid
in 3 soft bamboo baby yarns
and a metallic copper strand
with two strands of clear
copper-lined 6/0 beads

Destined to become a
necklace that is half beaded
and half plain braid

Beaded Braids

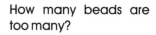

How many beads are too many?

It depends upon how important it is to be able to admire the kumihimo thread pattern. The more beads you have, the less braid is visible.

The top braid shown here has four strands of beads, the middle three each used two strands, and the bottom green strand has one strand of beads.

It is possible to put beads on every strand, but it isn't easy to keep your braid smooth. I found that the size 6/0 seed beads (e-beads) were too large to be used with embroidery floss in a successful 8-strand braid where all strands contained beads. You might enjoy experimenting with different sizes of cords and beads until you are happy with your result.

It's simple to braid an inch of a combination to see how it will look, then undo it and make adjustments. Try size 8/0 with embroidery thread for a narrower beaded cord.

You are still able to sew a focal bead onto the necklace or bracelet with matching thread.

2 strands of beads

Jewelry Gallery

Kumihimo Jewelry

Wearable Art

The braids in this book are all by the author.

All accessories and pendants are from her personal collection or are her own creations.

An Internet search should locate the various artists if you are interested in more information about them.
Most of the pendants are handmade, one-of-a-kind pieces.

8-strand round braid in shades of brown embroidery floss plus one metallic silver. Peruvian gourd pendant from the annual Chehaw Native American Cultural Festival in Georgia, 2006.

Round braid using 8 cords; including a soft tie-dye cotton and a metallic copper cord. Dichroic glass fused by Kathy James.

Kumihimo Jewelry　　　　Artistic Uses

Bracelet in 8-strand round braid with 2 strands of copper-lined size 6/0 seed beads; copper metallic embroidery floss, and 3 colors of soft silk and bamboo baby yarn. Matching necklace on page 82.

Scalloped 8-strand round braid using colors from the horned toad: light and dark turquoise, rust, metallic silver, and black embroidery floss, plus one strand of twisted denim-colored satin braid; by Kathy James. Exquisite Fimo clay horned toad by well-known clay artist Jon Anderson, residing in Bali.

4-strand round braid
with two strands of size 6 seed beads
and glass leaf pendant with foil
from Fire Mountain Gems.

Kumihimo Jewelry

Round braid using 8 strands; embroidery floss in a light mint, a medium mint, and a metallic silver, plus a black silk/bamboo yarn. Glass lampwork snake pendant by unknown catalog artist.

Round braid using 8 strands of embroidery floss in periwinkle blue, chartreuse, marine green, and metallic pastels. Borosilicate lampwork pendant by Earthworks Studios in Oregon.

Round braid using 8 strands; chenille, satin rope, variegated twisted ribbon, and black eyelash yarn.

Hand formed brass frog was purchased from an unknown artist at the annual Renaissance Festival in Larkspur, Colorado, 10 or more years ago.

Kumihimo Jewelry

Round braid using 8 strands; earth tones tie-dyed ribbon, eyelash yarn, and black satin rattail cord.
Braid and fused glass pendant by Kathy James.

Round braid using 4 strands of tie-dyed rainbow colored ribbon and 4 strands of black satin rattail.

Round braid using 16 strands of embroidery floss in lime green, parrot blue, purple, teal, and metallic pastels.
Braid and fused dichroic pendant by Kathy James.
Turquoise and silver pendant by unknown artist in Colorado Springs, Colorado.

Kumihimo Jewelry   **Artistic Uses**

8-strand round
braid using 6 black
satin rattail and
2 tie-dye cottons.
Onyx and silver
pendant from an
unknown vendor
at the 2006
Tucson Bead Show.

8-strand spiral round braid using
several shades of brown floss and
one metallic silver strand.
Unusual lampwork milkglass pendant
by Kristen Frantzen-Orr.

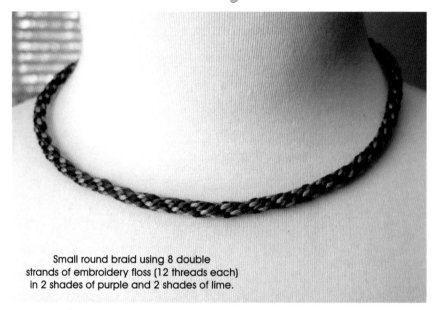

Small round braid using 8 double
strands of embroidery floss (12 threads each)
in 2 shades of purple and 2 shades of lime.

Very narrow round braid using
16 single threads of embroidery floss.
Polymer clay leaves on gourd disc
by Kathy James.

Kumihimo Jewelry

8-strand round braid
tie-dye cotton, rust and
purple embroidery floss,
metallic copper floss.
Borosilicate glass pendant
with imbedded opal
by Rashan Omari Jones
of New Mexico.

Plump and silky round braid using 8 strands
of 2mm satin rattail in two colors.

Kumihimo Jewelry

Half Beaded

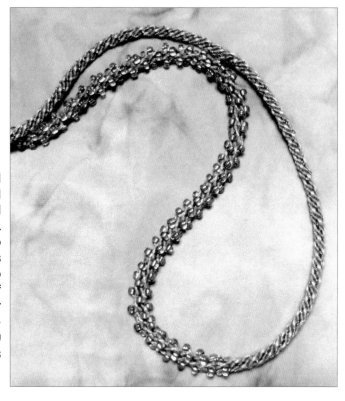

8-strand beaded braid in soft silk & bamboo baby yarns with two strands of clear copper-lined 6/0 e-beads

Round braid using 16 strands; in SW colors of embroidery floss; silver-lined brown seed beads.

8-strand beaded braid
in shades of green & purple
embroidery thread, with
two strands of deep plum
iridescent 6/0 e-beads.
Lampwork pendant
artist unknown.

Round braid using 8 strands;
purple organza, emerald
chenille, tie dye ribbon,
purple satin mousetail;
all cords and foil leaf glass
pendant are from
Fire Mountain Gems.

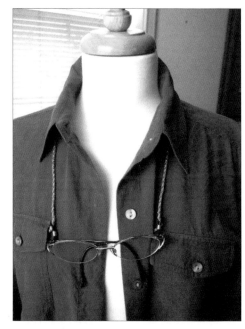

Eyeglass cords to match every outfit.

Pet leashes or collars

Other Kumihimo Uses

Matching zipper pull for a tapestry sewing bag.

Elegant, but simple, bookmark for a vintage volume

Shoelaces

Colorful and unique package ties.

Kumihimo on Gourds

Gourd artists are finding these lovely braids a new and colorful source of rim material for coiling. They make contemporary handles for purses, baskets, and canteens.

I hope you have found these instructions interesting, fun, and easy to follow.

If, when you are working with them, you have questions, or would like to make constructive suggestions for future books, please don't hesitate to let me know.

I hope you enjoy the creative art of modern kumihimo as much as I do.

Thanks,

Kathy James

Visit the author's website for Kumihimo Supplies
www.PrimitiveOriginals.com
KumiLooms and other disks, bobbins, decorative cords,
clamps/weights, kumihimo instructional books, endcaps, kits, size 6/0
seed beads, needles, free video instructions, etc.